W9-CPK-408

BEGINNING

SIGN
LANGUAGE

SERIES

Mother Goose in Sign

by S. Harold Collins

Illustrated by Kathy Kifer and Dahna Solar

Special thanks to the Larson Family
for their help and knowledge.

Published by
Garlic Press
605 Powers St.
Eugene, OR 97402

ISBN 0-931993-66-0
Order No. GP-066

www.garlicpress.com

Mother Goose In Sign presents traditional Mother Goose nursery rhymes fully illustrated in Signed English.

Enjoy not only the whole rhyme but realize that *One, Two, Buckle My Shoe* teaches numbers, *Solomon Grundy* teaches days of the week, and *Thirty Days Has September* teaches months.

Most vocabulary is standard Signed English, but there are some liberties with signs to accommodate the language of aged rhymes—stile (fence ladder), sixpence (six penny), gander (male goose).

- Solomon Grundy
- Thirty Days Has September
- One, Two, Buckle My Shoe
- Old Mother Goose
- The Crooked Sixpence

Solomon Grundy

Solomon Grundy,

born | on | Monday, | christened

on | Tuesday, | married | on

Wednesday, | became | ill | on

Thursday,

worse

on

Friday,

died

on

Saturday,

buried

on

Sunday.

This

is

the

end

of

Solomon Grundy.

Thirty Days
Has September

Thirty	days	has	September,
April,	June,	and	November;
February	has	twenty-eight	alone,

All	the	rest	have
thirty-one,	except	leap-year,	that
is	the	time	when
February	has	twenty-nine.	

One, Two, Buckle My Shoe

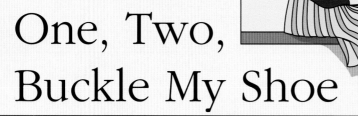

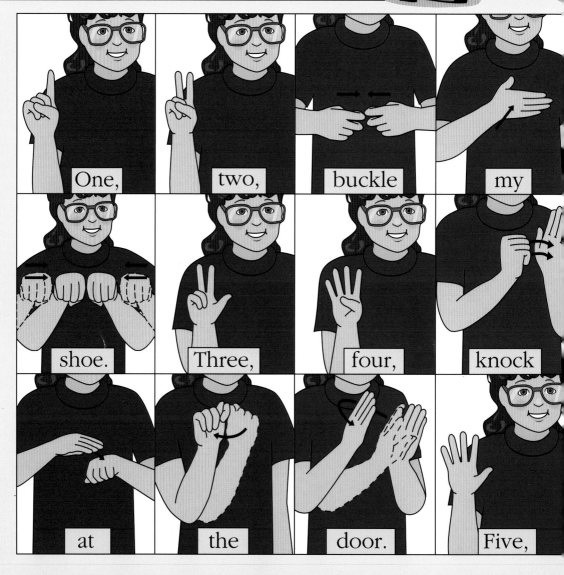

One, two, buckle my shoe. Three, four, knock at the door. Five,

six,	pick up	sticks.	Seven,
eight,	lay	them	straight.
Nine,	ten,	a	good,
fat	hen.	Eleven,	twelve,

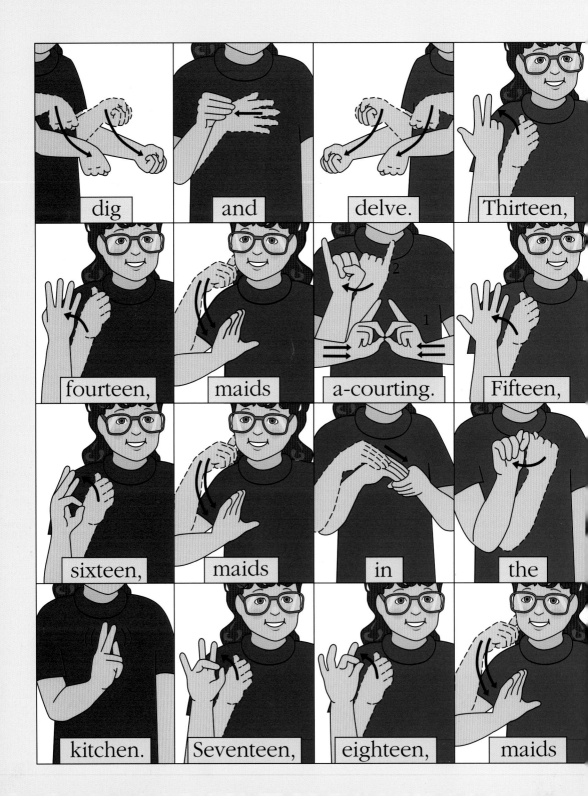

dig | and | delve. | Thirteen,

fourteen, | maids | a-courting. | Fifteen,

sixteen, | maids | in | the

kitchen. | Seventeen, | eighteen, | maids

a-waiting. Nineteen, twenty, my

plate is empty.

Old Mother Goose

| Old | Mother | Goose, | when |

she | wanted | to | wander,

would | ride | through | the

air | on | a | very

fine | gander.

The Crooked Sixpence

There

was

a

crooked

man,

and

he

walked

a

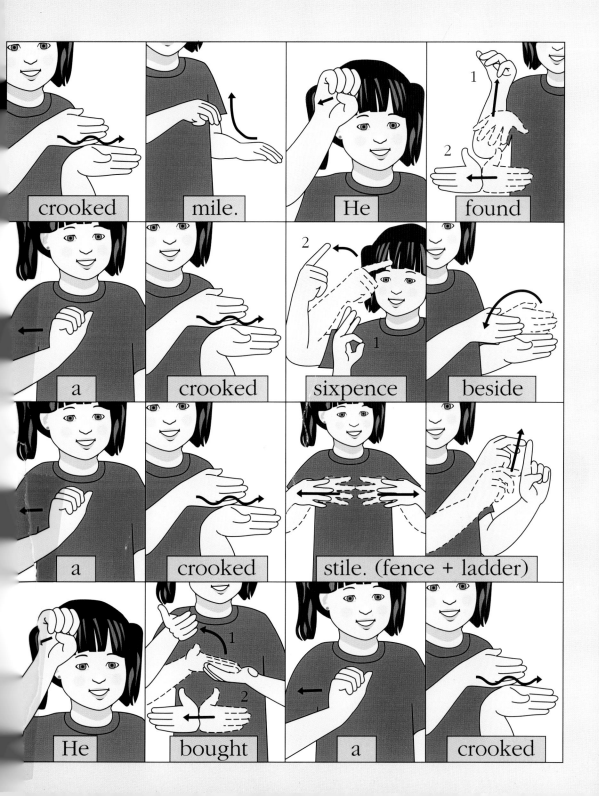

crooked	mile.	He	found
a	crooked	sixpence	beside
a	crooked	stile. (fence + ladder)	
He	bought	a	crooked

cat,	which	caught	a
crooked	mouse	and	they
all	lived	together	in
a	little	crooked	house.